LET'S VISIT...

WALES

Annabelle Lynch

W
FRANKLIN WATTS
LONDON • SYDNEY

First published in 2015 by
Franklin Watts
338 Euston Road
London NW1 3BH

Franklin Watts Australia
Level 17/207 Kent Street
Sydney NSW 2000
© 2015 Franklin Watts

HB ISBN 978 1 4451 3704 9
Library eBook ISBN: 978 1 4451 3705 6

Dewey classification number: 942

A CIP catalogue record for
this book is available from the
British Library.

Editor: Julia Bird
Designer: Jeni Child

Printed in China

Photo acknowledgements: antb/
Shutterstock: 1, 4-5. Phillip Bird LRPS CPAGB/
Shutterstock: 5t, 10, 11tr. Tom Brindley/
Shutterstock: 15b. Matthew Dixon
/Shutterstock: 3bl, 20-21. Glyn Evans/
PhotoLibrary Wales/Alamy: 21bl. Len Green/
Shutterstock: 18. Phil Holden/Alamy: 9t. David
Hosking/FLPA: 19b. Chris Howes/Wild Places
Photography/Alamy: 17t, 17b. Gail Johnson/
Shutterstock: 5b, 6b, 14. Warren Kovach/
Alamy: 19t. Steve Liptrot/Dreamstime: 12.
Steve Lovegrove/Shutterstock: 16t. Manor
Photography/Alamy: 9b. Jeff Morgan 03/
Alamy: 3br, 13t. Roger Nicol/Shutterstock: 4c.
Michael Olivers/Alamy: 21br. Steve Pleydell/
PhotoLibrary Wales/Shutterstock: 2,
8t. Ronigs/Dreamstime: front cover. Mark
Salter/Alamy: 15t. Samot/Shutterstock:
7t. tazzymoto/Shutterstock: 16b. Simon
Tilley/Alamy: 13b. travelibeurope/Alamy:
11b. Tosca Weijers/Dreamstime: 7c. Steve
Wilson/Shutterstock: 11t. Bahadir Yeniceri/
Dreamstime: 7b.

Every attempt has been made
to clear copyright. Should there
be any inadvertent omission,
please apply to the Publishers for
rectification.

Franklin Watts is a division of
Hachette Children's Books,
an Hachette UK company.
www.hachette.co.uk

CONTENTS

Words in **bold** are in the glossary.

LET'S VISIT
WALES

Wales lies to the far west of the United Kingdom. It shares a long land **border** with England in the east. The rest of Wales is surrounded by sea.

Porthmelgan Beach can be found on Wales' west coast.

What does it look like?

Wales has a long, dramatic coastline with high cliffs and sandy beaches. There are lots of mountains in the middle and the north of the country, with deep lakes and tumbling waterfalls.

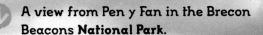
A view from Pen y Fan in the Brecon Beacons **National Park.**

In the city

The **capital** city of Wales is Cardiff. It is found in the south-east corner of Wales. Other cities include Swansea and Newport.

Cardiff city centre on a sunny afternoon.

When to go

Wales has warm summers and mild winters. The sunny late spring and summer months are usually the best times to visit, but pack a raincoat as it can rain a lot, especially during the winter.

Clouds gather off the coast of the island of Anglesey in north Wales.

TRAVEL TIP

The Welsh language is alive and well in Wales. Look out for Welsh words on road signs!

CONWY CASTLE

Wales is famous for its many castles, and Conwy Castle is one of the most spectacular of them all.

Town and castle

Conwy Castle lies on the north coast of Wales, in the old walled town of Conwy. The River Conwy flows close by, giving the town and the castle their name.

TRAVEL TIP

Take a walk around Conwy's town walls with their 21 towers for great views over the town.

Conwy Castle was built close to an important crossing of the River Conwy.

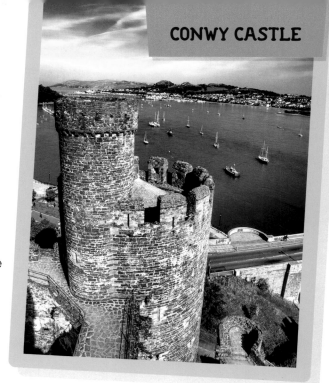

CONWY CASTLE

England invade

Conwy Castle was built more than 700 years ago by the English King Edward I. He wanted to take control over all of Wales and built the castle as a **fortress** to guard the town of Conwy. For many years, Welsh people could not even enter Conwy.

The view from one of Conwy Castle's famous towers.

A grand castle

Today, anyone can explore mighty Conwy Castle! You can climb right to the top of its eight huge towers and walk around the Great Hall, kitchen and king's and queen's rooms. It's fun to imagine what life would have been like for the people who lived there.

A model soldier guards Conwy Castle's entrance.

OTHER PLACES TO SEE IN **CONWY:**

Great Britain's smallest house (right)

Conwy Bridge

Bodnant Garden

THE GOWER PENINSULA

Three Cliffs Bay is one of the best beaches on the Gower Peninsula.

Stretching for over 30 kilometres along the coast of South Wales, the Gower Peninsula is a wondeful place to visit in Wales.

Protected place

Gower was the first place in the UK to be made an Area of Outstanding Natural Beauty. This means that its beautiful **landscape** is strictly protected. In the south, it has wide, white beaches and rocky cliffs with dark caves. In the north you can see **dunes** and **marshes**. Away from the coast, there are rolling woodlands.

TRAVEL TIP

Langland Bay is a great place to explore rockpools at low tide.

Take to the waves on a bodyboard!

 ## Things to do

There are lots of fun things to do in Gower. You can paddle, swim or even surf at many of Gower's beaches, or just have fun building sandcastles. There are lots of good cycle rides and walks to try, too. When the tide is low, you can walk out to the island at Worm's Head to see the seals sleeping on the rocks. If all that walking has tired you out, have fun on a pony trek along the beach.

A pony trek is a great way to see Gower's beautiful beaches.

THREE GREAT BEACHES TO TRY:

Rhossili Bay

Pobbles Bay

Horton

WELSH MOUNTAIN ZOO

Meet the animals at the Welsh Mountain Zoo!

Home in the hills

The Welsh Mountain Zoo is perched high on a hill in north Wales, overlooking the seaside town of Colwyn Bay. It opened in 1963 and now welcomes around 200,000 visitors every year.

OTHER GREAT **ZOOS** AND **AQUARIUMS:**

Manor House Wildlife Park

Anglesey Sea Zoo

Folly Zoo

You can meet the fierce-looking Harris' hawk at the Welsh Mountain Zoo.

Don't miss seeing the rare and beautiful snow leopards.

Cotton-top tamarins are only found in the wild in the forests of Colombia.

About the animals

The zoo brings together animals from all over the world, from camels to chimpanzees and from scarlet macaws to Mississippi alligators. You shouldn't miss seeing the pair of **endangered** snow leopards or the **rare** cotton-top tamarins.

Meet the animals

The zoo has lots of great ways for you to get up close with the animals. Take part in a training session with the fun-loving sealions, march with the Penguin Parade or just cuddle the rabbits at the Children's Farm.

TRAVEL TIP

Don't miss the Tarzan Trail Adventure playground.

Watch the marching penguins get a fishy reward!

BIG PIT NATIONAL COAL MUSEUM

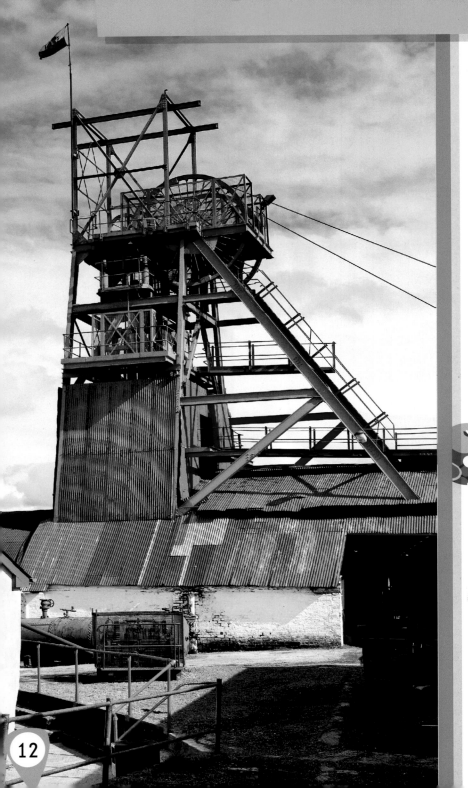

Visit Big Pit National Coal Museum in Torfaen, South Wales to find out all about the world of mining.

Precious coal

Wales has a long history of **coal mining**. In the past, the mining **industry** provided many jobs and brought lots of money to Wales. Today, there are only a few small mines left in Wales.

The winding tower at Big Pit Coal Museum.

A former miner describes daily life at the mine to some visitors.

OTHER GREAT MUSEUMS TO SEE:

National Museum Cardiff

St Fagans National History Museum

National Waterfront Museum

Deep down

At Big Pit, you can travel deep under the ground on a tour with real ex-miners. You will learn how mining is done and wear a helmet with a lamp on it, just like a real miner.

You can see old equipment that all miners carried in the store room.

Find out more

You can find out more about the history of coal mining in Wales in the museum. You can explore old mining buildings, such as the blacksmith's **forge**, baths and canteen, and discover what life was like in the past for Wales' hardworking miners, many of whom were only children.

TRAVEL TIP

Mines can be dangerous. Before you go on the underground tour, your guide will collect anything that could start a fire, such as mobile phones and cameras.

SNOWDONIA

Reaching 1,085 metres into the sky, Snowdon is the highest mountain in Wales and the tallest point in the UK outside Scotland.

Up and down

Snowdon is found in the beautiful Snowdonia National Park in north Wales. Millions of people head there every year, and around 450,000 of them go on to climb mighty Snowdon. There are six main paths up the mountain, and a trip up and back down the mountain takes around five to six hours. On the way you will see rocky cliffs, rare mountain plants and clear lakes.

Mount Snowdon is often covered with snow.

 Snowdon is known as the UK's busiest mountain!

TRAVEL TIP

Always take care when walking in the mountains, and keep to the path at all times.

Take the train

If walking isn't for you, have an exciting ride on the Snowdon Mountain Railway. This train line has been running for over a hundred years. It starts in the village of Llanberis at the foot of Snowdon and climbs all the way to the snowy top of the mountain – a journey of around 7 kilometres. The views are amazing!

GREAT PLACES TO VISIT IN
SNOWDONIA:

Portmeirion

GreenWood Forest Park

Llechwedd Slate Caverns

 The Snowdon train sets off on its journey back to the bottom of Mount Snowdon.

ST FAGANS

Are you interested in the history of Wales?
Visit St Fagans National History Museum
in Cardiff to find out all about it.

St Teilo's Church was built between 1100 and 1520. It took 20 years to move it to St Fagans.

 ## Life in the past

St Fagans is an amazing open-air museum which brings together over forty different buildings from Wales' past, from schoolhouses to bakeries. These have been carefully rebuilt at St Fagans to give visitors a true picture of how all kinds of Welsh people used to live.

The tiny post office looks exactly the same as it would have looked in 1940.

The forge at St Fagans. Lots of metal tools would have been made here.

TRAVEL TIP

St Fagans celebrates different Welsh festivals, such as St David's Day, with special food, music and dance. Look out for one!

See for yourself

Walk around St Fagans and the history of Wales comes to life around you. See a blacksmith at work in the forge, watch woollen blankets and shawls being made in the mill and see **potters**, tailors and **clog**-makers hard at work. In the nearby fields, you can watch farmers look after their cows, pigs and sheep. If you're getting hungry after all that, try a Welsh cake from the traditional bakehouse!

OTHER GREAT PLACES TO GO **NEARBY:**

Castell Coch

Llandaff Cathedral

Bute Park

The grocery at St Fagans displays the kind of food that was for sale in the 1920s.

17

ANGLESEY SEA ZOO

The Menai Bridge carries cars over the Menai Strait. It opened in 1826.

Explore Wales' underwater world at Anglesey Sea Zoo.

Island home

Anglesey is a big island which lies off the north-west coast of Wales. You can reach it by crossing the Menai Bridge. Anglesey Sea Zoo is one of the island's top places to visit.

Meet the sea creatures

The zoo is home to over 150 different **species** of sea creatures found around the Welsh coast, including sharks, eels, octopuses, seals and lobsters. You can meet them in the Kelp Forest, Shark Pools and Lobster Hatchery. Daily talks and feeding times will help you find out more about our fishy friends, while a Sea Safari will even take you out on the nearby ocean to spot sea creatures!

Get up close with the fish at the Big Fish Forest.

Helping hand

Anglesey Sea Zoo works hard to protect sea creatures. As well as **breeding** creatures such as seahorses at the zoo, workers also rescue sick or injured seals, dolphins, whales, turtles and sea birds, and help them to get better.

Common dolphins swim in the sea off the Welsh coast.

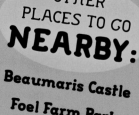

OTHER PLACES TO GO
NEARBY:

Beaumaris Castle

Foel Farm Park

Anglesey Riding Centre

TRAVEL TIP

Don't miss the adventure playground and giant bouncy castle!

CARDIFF BAY

Cardiff Bay is a big waterfront development, stretching for around 10 kilometres along the coast of Cardiff.

GREAT PLACES TO VISIT IN CARDIFF:

The Millennium Stadium

Cardiff Castle

National Museum, Cardiff

New life

Cardiff had been a busy **port** since the 19th century, but by the 1980s the port was used less and less. Cardiff's **dockland** became empty. People decided to give the area new life. A **barrage** placed across the bay created a big lake there, fed by the nearby rivers Ely and Taff, and lots of new buildings were built.

 The lake at Cardiff Bay, lit up at night.

 TRAVEL TIP

Roald Dahl Plass, named after the famous author who was born in Cardiff, is a great place to see concerts and festivals. It has even featured in *Doctor Who*!

Waterside fun

Today, Cardiff Bay has lots to offer for everyone. You can go on boat tours of the bay, visit the science and discovery centre Techniquest, which also includes a great **planetarium**, or go bird-spotting at the Cardiff Bay Wetland Reserve. You can even go on a guided tour of the Cardiff Bay Barrage itself. Or you can just relax with an ice cream in one of the many waterfront cafes, enjoying the beautiful views.

 Swans and other wild birds gather at the Wetland Reserve.

Have fun while learning about the world around us at Techniquest.

21

MAP OF WALES

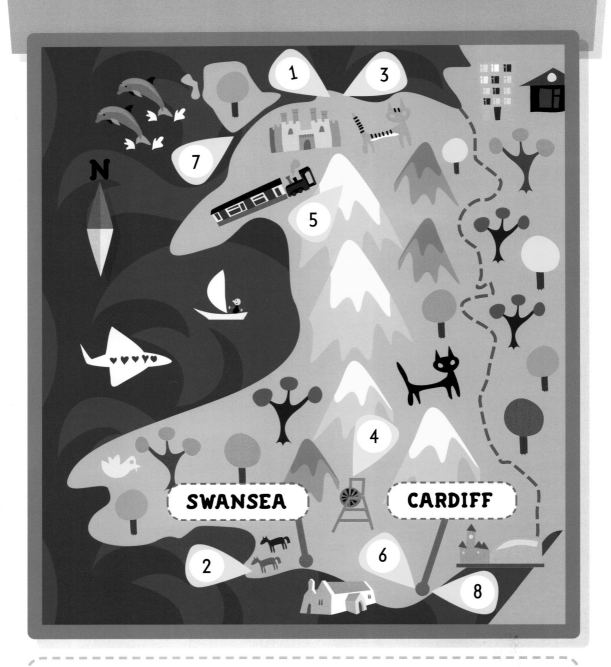

SWANSEA

CARDIFF

N

KEY:
1 Conwy Castle
2 The Gower Peninsula
3 Welsh Mountain Zoo
4 Big Pit National Coal Museum
5 Snowdonia
6 St Fagans
7 Anglesey Sea Zoo
8 Cardiff Bay

GLOSSARY

barrage
A barrier across a stretch of water, such as a river or lake

border
A line that divides two countries

breed
To have babies together

capital
The city where a country's government meets

clog
A type of wooden shoe

coal mining
Digging coal out from under the Earth's surface

dockland
The area around ship docks

dune
A hill made of sand

endangered
At risk of dying out

forge
A place where metal is shaped

fortress
A castle or other strong building that is difficult for enemies to enter

grocery
A shop that sells food and household items

industry
Business or work

landscape
Everything you can see when you look at an area, such as hills, forests, rivers and buildings

marsh
A low, damp area of land

national park
A protected area of countryside that people can visit

peninsula
A long, narrow piece of land that sticks out into the sea

planetarium
A big room in which the planets and stars are shown on a rounded ceiling

port
A place by the sea from where boats and ships arrive and depart

potter
Someone who makes pottery, such as plates, cups and pots, from clay

rare
Something that is not often seen

species
A group of animals, such as dogs, that share many things in common and can breed together

INDEX

FURTHER INFORMATION

Books

Fact Cat: Wales by Alice Harman (Wayland, 2014)

Living in the UK: Wales by Annabelle Lynch (Franklin Watts, 2014)

Websites

http://www.welshmountainzoo.org

www.museumwales.ac.uk/bigpit/

www.museumwales.ac.uk/stfagans

Every effort has been made by the Publishers to ensure that the websites are suitable for children, and that they contain no inappropriate or offensive material. However, because of the nature of the Internet, it is impossible to guarantee that the contents of these sites will not be altered. We strongly advise that Internet access is supervised by a responsible adult.